C000063645

# Practical
# Soups

$p^3$

This is a P³ Book
This edition published in 2003

P³
Queen Street House
4 Queen Street
Bath BA1 1HE, UK

Copyright © Parragon 2002

All rights reserved. No part of this publication may be reproduced, stored
in a retrieval system or transmitted, in any form or by any means, electronic,
mechanical, photocopying, recording or otherwise, without the prior permission
of the copyright holder.

ISBN: 1-40540-553-8

Printed in China

**NOTE**

This book uses metric and imperial measurements. Follow the same units
of measurement throughout; do not mix metric and imperial.
All spoon measurements are level: teaspoons are assumed to be 5 ml, and
tablespoons are assumed to be 15 ml. Unless otherwise stated,
milk is assumed to be full fat, eggs and individual vegetables such as potatoes
are medium, and pepper is freshly ground black pepper.

The nutritional information provided for each recipe is per serving or per person.
Optional ingredients, variations or serving suggestions have
not been included in the calculations. The times given for each recipe are an approximate
guide only because the preparation times may differ according to the techniques used by
different people and the cooking times may vary as a result of the type of oven used.

Recipes using raw or very lightly cooked eggs should be
avoided by children, the elderly, pregnant women, convalescents,
and anyone suffering from an illness.

# Contents

# Introduction

The traditional way to start a meal is with a soup, but soups can also provide satisfying meals by themselves. They are quick and easy to prepare, provide a filling, healthy meal, and can be made from an almost infinite number of ingredients and with a wonderful range of international flavours. From a Spanish Tomato Soup or Chinese Wonton Soup, to an Italian Minestrone or a Louisiana Seafood Gumbo, you are sure to find a soup in this book to suit any occasion. This book presents recipes that are quick and simple to prepare, yet which will provide healthy, tasty dishes for you, your family and your guests.

## Stock

For the best results, use home-made stock as the base for your soup. Use liquor left from cooking vegetables and the juices from cooking fish and meat to make the best stock. In this way your soup will be rich in vitamins and nutrients from the cooked food – and remember it can easily be frozen in small amounts and used the next time you are making soup. Ready-made stock cubes are an alternative to fresh stock if you are short of time, but be careful because the strong flavourings they contain can easily overpower delicate dishes and they also tend to be very salty.

## History

Soup was first made ten thousand years ago when the Egyptians prepared it by boiling ingredients in a large clay pot over an open fire; they served the soup in shells or horns. Since then the popularity of soups has soared. Indeed, the Baulangers Inn in Paris, the forerunner of all restaurants, had nothing but soup on its menu. Today, the range of soups has widened vastly and cooking methods and recipes have completely changed. Soup, however, has continued to be an all-time favourite.

Most soups are very nutritious, especially those that have a high vegetable content, while being inexpensive and filling. In fact, these are the reasons why soup has been served in soup kitchens for many years. Surprisingly perhaps, it was Al Capone who founded and funded the first soup kitchen as a charitable organisation in Chicago in the 1930s. He actually paid $350 per day from his own finances to feed as many as 3,000 unemployed people. It has been suggested, however, that his actions were motivated not by human kindness but instead by the fact that he wanted to prevent people from revealing the secrets of his criminal activities.

## International specialities

Soup is generally extremely easy to make, because it is simply a process of boiling a combination of meats, fish or vegetables together in order to obtain the desired consistency. Certain soups have even become renowned as national specialities.

Soup is very popular in Italy, where key ingredients vary from region to region. In northern Italy, soups are based on rice, while in Tuscany, thick bean or bread-based soups are popular. In southern Italy, tomato, garlic and pasta soups are favoured. Minestrone is the most well-known Italian soup and is now made worldwide, with arguably the best version coming from Milan. The best Italian soups are produced in coastal fishing villages.

Soup is an integral part of the Chinese meal too, but is more frequently served as a main course or to clear the palate between courses instead of as a starter. Chinese soups are frequently clear but contain wontons, dumplings, noodles or rice to add texture and flavour.

Borscht originates from Eastern Europe and is particularly popular in Poland and Russia. Its popularity may be due in part to its vivid red colour caused by its

main ingredient: beetroot. Borscht was introduced to France by Russian emigrants in the 1920s and has now become an established favourite. Variations of the original Borscht have evolved to produce other quick, simple and healthy beetroot soups.

Perhaps the most famous of the French soups – aside from French Onion – is Vichyssoise. A popular favourite, it was originally a leek and potato soup created by a French chef working in America. It is usually served cold, thickened with fresh cream and garnished with chives. Today the term Vichyssoise is used to refer to any cold potato-based soup made with other vegetables, such as courgettes.

The Spanish also have a traditional soup, which is called Gazpacho. Traditionally served ice-cold, it is made from cucumber, tomato, red pepper, breadcrumbs, garlic and olive oil. Preparation varies between regions throughout Spain: in Jerez for example, it is served garnished with raw onions, whereas in Cádiz it is served hot in winter.

Gazpacho and Vichyssoise are not the only soups that can be served cold. Chilled fruit soups are ideal for summer lunches or for light evening meals when served with a sandwich or salad. Garnishing with croûtons, grated cheese or soured cream often enhances the flavour of the soup and also improves its presentation.

## Commonly used terms

Here are some commonly used terms that are often encountered in relation to soups.

**Bisque**: this soup is made with puréed shellfish, fresh cream and Cognac. It evolved from a boiled game or meat soup to one made with pigeon or quail, until crayfish became established as the key ingredient in the seventeenth century.

**Bouillabaisse**: now commonly associated with expensive restaurants, this dish was originally prepared on the beach by fishermen who boiled together scraps of unsaleable fish with herbs to form a hearty meal. The word 'bouillabaisse' more correctly describes this form of cooking, which means to boil rapidly and reduce. Almost any fish, including shellfish, can be used to make bouillabaisse, although oily fish such as sardines and mackerel should be avoided. Traditionally the soup and the fish are served separately, with the soup poured over dried, home-made bread. Today the bread is frequently replaced with garlic croûtons.

**Chowder**: this term, which originated in North America or Canada, describes a clam or fish soup so thick that is it is almost a stew.

**Consommé**: this clear soup is formed from meat, fish or poultry stock. It can be served hot or cold and can be garnished with thinly sliced meat, vermicelli, vegetables, bone marrow, poached eggs, cheese or croûtons. Cold consommé may appear gelatinous; this is caused by the concentration of nutritive elements.

**Gumbo**: this soup, which originated in Louisiana, is a particular favourite in North America and Canada. The okra pods traditionally used in its preparation thicken the mixture so that the resultant dish is almost a stew.

**Purée**: this term is generally used to describe any thick soup where the ingredients have in part been blended or cooked until very soft. It is the starch from the puréed vegetables that thickens the soup.

**Stock**: now available as granules or ready-made preparations, this unclarified broth is obtained by boiling fish, meat and/or vegetables. It is used instead of water for preparing soups and sauces.

**Velouté**: these are generally soups that have been thickened with egg yolks, butter and/or cream.

| KEY | |
|---|---|
|  | Simplicity level 1–3 (1 easiest, 3 slightly harder) |
|  | Preparation time |
|  | Cooking time |

# Avocado & Mint Soup

This is a rich and creamy pale-green soup made with avocados and enhanced by a touch of mint. Serve chilled in summer or hot in winter.

## NUTRITIONAL INFORMATION

| | | |
|---|---|---|
| Calories .......199 | Sugars ..........3g |
| Protein .........3g | Fat ..........18g |
| Carbohydrate ....7g | Saturates .......6g |

🍃

🥗 15 mins  🕐 35 mins

### SERVES 6

## I N G R E D I E N T S

3 tbsp butter or margarine

6 spring onions, sliced

1 garlic clove, crushed

4 tbsp plain flour

600 ml/1 pint vegetable stock

2 ripe avocados

2–3 tsp lemon juice

pinch of grated lemon zest

150 ml/5 fl oz milk

150 ml/5 fl oz single cream

1–1½ tbsp chopped fresh mint

salt and pepper

sprigs of fresh mint, to garnish

## M I N T E D   G A R L I C   B R E A D

100 g/3½ oz butter

1–2 tbsp chopped fresh mint

1–2 garlic cloves, crushed

1 stick wholemeal or white French bread

1 Melt the butter or margarine in a large, heavy-based saucepan. Add the spring onions and garlic and cook over a low heat, stirring occasionally, for about 3 minutes until soft and translucent.

2 Stir in the flour and cook, stirring, for 1–2 minutes. Gradually stir in the stock, then bring to the boil. Simmer gently while preparing the avocados.

3 Peel the avocados, discard the stones and chop coarsely. Add to the soup with the lemon juice and zest and the seasoning. Cover and simmer for about 10 minutes until tender.

4 Cool the soup slightly, then press through a sieve with the back of a spoon or process in a food processor or blender to a smooth purée. Pour the soup into a bowl.

5 Stir in the milk and cream, adjust the seasoning, then stir in the mint. Cover and chill thoroughly.

6 To make the minted garlic bread, soften the butter and beat in the mint and garlic. Cut the loaf into slanting slices but leave a hinge on the bottom crust. Spread each slice with the butter and reassemble the loaf. Wrap in foil and place in a preheated oven, 180°C/350°F/Gas Mark 4, for about 15 minutes.

7 Serve the soup garnished with a sprig of mint and accompanied by the minted garlic bread.

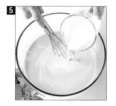

# Potato & Split Pea Soup

Split green peas are sweeter than other varieties of split pea and reduce down to a purée when cooked, which acts as a thickener in soups.

## NUTRITIONAL INFORMATION

| | |
|---|---|
| Calories . . . . . . .260 | Sugars . . . . . . . . .5g |
| Protein . . . . . . . .11g | Fat . . . . . . . . . .10g |
| Carbohydrate . . .32g | Saturates . . . . . . .3g |

 5–10 mins  45 mins

### SERVES 4

## I N G R E D I E N T S

2 tbsp vegetable oil

2 large, unpeeled floury potatoes, diced

2 onions, diced

75 g/2¾ oz split green peas

1 litre/1¾ pints vegetable stock

60 g/2¼ oz Gruyère, grated

salt and pepper

### C R O U T O N S

3 tbsp butter

1 garlic clove, crushed

1 tbsp chopped fresh parsley

1 thick slice white bread, cubed

1 Heat the vegetable oil in a large saucepan. Add the potatoes and onions and sauté over a low heat, stirring constantly, for about 5 minutes.

2 Add the split green peas to the pan and stir together well.

3 Pour the vegetable stock into the pan and bring to the boil. Reduce the heat to low and simmer for 35 minutes until the potatoes are tender and the split peas are cooked.

4 Meanwhile, make the croûtons. Melt the butter in a frying pan. Add the garlic, parsley and bread cubes and cook,

turning frequently, for 2 minutes until the bread cubes are golden brown on all sides.

5 Stir the grated cheese into the soup and season to taste with salt and pepper. Heat gently until the cheese is starting to melt.

6 Pour the soup into warmed individual bowls and sprinkle the croûtons on top. Serve at once.

### VARIATION

For a richly coloured soup, red lentils could be used instead of split green peas. Add a large pinch of brown sugar to the recipe for extra sweetness if red lentils are used.

# Avocado & Vegetable Soup

Avocado has a rich flavour and colour and makes a creamy-textured soup. It is best served chilled, but may be eaten warm as well.

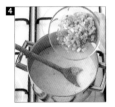

### NUTRITIONAL INFORMATION

| | | | |
|---|---|---|---|
| Calories | ......167 | Sugars | .........5g |
| Protein | .........4g | Fat | ..........13g |
| Carbohydrate | ....8g | Saturates | .......3g |

 15 mins    ⊕ 10 mins

### SERVES 4

## I N G R E D I E N T S

1 large, ripe avocado

2 tbsp lemon juice

1 tbsp vegetable oil

125 g/4½ oz canned sweetcorn, drained

2 tomatoes, skinned and deseeded

1 garlic clove, crushed

1 leek, chopped

1 red chilli, chopped

400 ml/14 fl oz vegetable stock

150 ml/5 fl oz milk

shredded leek, to garnish

### COOK'S TIP

If serving chilled, transfer from the food processor to a bowl, and stir in the vegetable stock, milk and reserved vegetables. Cover and refrigerate for at least 4 hours.

1 Peel the avocado and mash the flesh with a fork, stir in the lemon juice and reserve until required.

2 Heat the oil in a large saucepan. Add the sweetcorn, tomatoes, garlic, leek and chilli and sauté over a low heat for 2–3 minutes or until softened.

3 Put half of the vegetable mixture in a food processor or blender, add the mashed avocado and process until smooth. Transfer the mixture to a clean saucepan.

4 Add the vegetable stock, milk and reserved vegetables and cook over a low heat for 3–4 minutes until hot. Transfer to warmed individual serving bowls, garnish with shredded leek and serve immediately.

# Spanish Tomato Soup

This Mediterranean tomato soup is thickened with bread, as is traditional in some parts of Spain, and served with garlic bread.

## NUTRITIONAL INFORMATION

| | | | |
|---|---|---|---|
| Calories | .......297 | Sugars | .........7g |
| Protein | .........8g | Fat | ..........13g |
| Carbohydrate | ...39g | Saturates | .......2g |

 10 mins     🕐 20 mins

### SERVES 4

## INGREDIENTS

4 tbsp olive oil

1 onion, chopped

3 garlic cloves, crushed

1 green pepper, deseeded and chopped

½ tsp chilli powder

500 g/1 lb 2 oz tomatoes, chopped

225 g/8 oz French or Italian bread, cubed

1 litre/1¾ pints vegetable stock

### GARLIC BREAD

4 slices ciabatta or French bread

4 tbsp olive oil

2 garlic cloves, crushed

25 g/1 oz Cheddar cheese, grated

chilli powder, to garnish

1 Heat the olive oil in a large frying pan. Add the onion, garlic and green pepper and sauté over a low heat, stirring frequently, for about 2–3 minutes or until the onion has softened.

2 Add the chilli powder and tomatoes and cook over a medium heat until the mixture has thickened.

3 Stir in the bread cubes and stock and cook for 10–15 minutes until the soup is thick and fairly smooth.

4 Meanwhile, make the garlic bread. Toast the bread slices under a medium grill. Drizzle the oil over the top of the bread, rub with the garlic, sprinkle over the cheese and return to the grill for 2–3 minutes until the cheese has melted. Sprinkle with chilli powder and serve with the soup.

### VARIATION

Replace the green pepper with red or orange pepper, if you prefer.

# Cauliflower & Broccoli Soup

Full of flavour, this creamy cauliflower and broccoli soup is simple to make and absolutely delicious to eat.

## NUTRITIONAL INFORMATION

Calories .......378  Sugars ........14g
Protein ........18g  Fat ..........26g
Carbohydrate ...20g  Saturates .......7g

 10 mins   35 mins

### SERVES 4

## I N G R E D I E N T S

3 tbsp vegetable oil

1 red onion, chopped

2 garlic cloves, crushed

300 g/10½ oz cauliflower florets

300 g/10½ oz broccoli florets

1 tbsp plain flour

600 ml/1 pint milk

300 ml/10 fl oz vegetable stock

75 g/2¾ oz Gruyère, grated

pinch of paprika

150 ml/5 fl oz single cream

### T O   G A R N I S H

Gruyère shavings

paprika

1 Heat the oil in a large, heavy-based saucepan. Add the onion, garlic, cauliflower and broccoli and sauté over a low heat, stirring constantly, for 3–4 minutes. Add the flour and cook, stirring constantly, for another minute.

2 Gradually stir in the milk and stock and bring to the boil, stirring constantly. Lower the heat and simmer for 20 minutes.

3 Remove about one-quarter of the vegetables with a slotted spoon and set aside. Put the remaining soup in a food processor or blender and process for about 30 seconds until smooth. Alternatively, press the vegetables through a sieve with the back of a wooden spoon. Transfer the soup to a clean saucepan.

4 Return the reserved vegetable pieces to the soup. Stir in the grated cheese, paprika and single cream and heat through over a low heat, without boiling, for 2–3 minutes or until the cheese starts to melt.

5 Transfer to warmed individual serving bowls, garnish with shavings of Gruyère and dust with paprika. Serve the soup immediately.

## COOK'S TIP

The soup must not start to boil after the cream has been added, otherwise it will curdle. Use natural yogurt instead of the cream if preferred, but again do not let it boil.

# Curried Parsnip Soup

Parsnips make a delicious soup because they have a slightly sweet flavour. In this recipe, spices are added to complement this sweetness.

| NUTRITIONAL INFORMATION | |
| --- | --- |
| Calories .......152 | Sugars .........7g |
| Protein .........3g | Fat ...........8g |
| Carbohydrate ...18g | Saturates .......3g |

10 mins    35 mins

**SERVES 4**

## I N G R E D I E N T S

1 tbsp vegetable oil

1 tbsp butter

1 red onion, chopped

3 parsnips, chopped

2 garlic cloves, crushed

2 tsp garam masala

½ tsp chilli powder

1 tbsp plain flour

150 ml/5 fl oz vegetable stock

grated rind and juice of 1 lemon

salt and pepper

strips of lemon rind, to garnish

1 Heat the oil and butter in a large saucepan until the butter has melted. Add the onion, parsnips and garlic and sauté, stirring frequently, for 5–7 minutes until the vegetables have softened but not coloured.

2 Add the garam masala and chilli powder and cook, stirring constantly, for 30 seconds. Sprinkle in the flour, mix well and cook, stirring constantly, for another 30 seconds.

3 Stir in the stock, lemon rind and lemon juice and bring to the boil. Lower the heat and simmer for 20 minutes.

4 Remove some of the vegetable pieces with a slotted spoon and reserve until required. Process the remaining soup and vegetables in a food processor or blender for about 1 minute to a smooth purée. Alternatively, put the vegetables in a sieve and press through with the back of a wooden spoon.

5 Return the soup to a clean saucepan and stir in the reserved vegetables. Heat the soup through for 2 minutes until piping hot.

6 Season to taste with salt and pepper then transfer to soup bowls. Garnish with strips of lemon rind and serve.

# Vegetable & Corn Chowder

This is a really filling soup, which should be served before a light main course. It is easy to prepare and is filled with flavour.

## NUTRITIONAL INFORMATION

| | | | |
|---|---|---|---|
| Calories | .......378 | Sugars | ........20g |
| Protein | ........16g | Fat | ..........13g |
| Carbohydrate | ...52g | Saturates | .......6g |

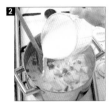

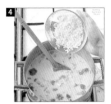

 15 mins    🕐 30 mins

### SERVES 4

## I N G R E·D·I E N T S

1 tbsp vegetable oil

1 red onion, diced

1 red pepper, deseeded and diced

3 garlic cloves, crushed

1 large potato, diced

2 tbsp plain flour

600 ml/1 pint milk

300 ml/10 fl oz vegetable stock

50 g/1¾ oz broccoli florets

675 g/1lb 8 oz canned sweetcorn, drained

75 g/2¾ oz Cheddar cheese, grated

salt and pepper

1 tbsp chopped fresh coriander, to garnish

## COOK'S TIP

If you are making this soup for a vegetarian, choose a vegetarian cheese, which is made with rennet of non-animal origin, using microbial or fungal enzymes.

1 Heat the oil in a large saucepan. Add the onion, red pepper, garlic and potato and sauté over a low heat, stirring frequently, for 2–3 minutes.

2 Stir in the flour and cook, stirring, for 30 seconds. Gradually stir in the milk and stock.

3 Add the broccoli florets and the sweetcorn. Bring the mixture to the boil, stirring constantly, then lower the heat and simmer for about 20 minutes or until all the vegetables are tender.

4 Add 50 g/1¼ oz of the cheese and stir until it melts.

5 Season and spoon the chowder into warm serving bowls. Garnish with the remaining cheese and the chopped coriander and serve.

# Vichyssoise

This is a classic creamy soup made from potatoes and leeks. To achieve the delicate pale colour, be sure to use only the white parts of the leeks.

## NUTRITIONAL INFORMATION

Calories . . . . . . .208   Sugars . . . . . . . . .5g
Protein . . . . . . . . .5g   Fat . . . . . . . . . .12g
Carbohydrate . . .20g   Saturates . . . . . . .6g

   10 mins      40 mins

### SERVES 6

## I N G R E D I E N T S

3 large leeks

3 tbsp butter or margarine

1 onion, thinly sliced

500 g/1 lb 2 oz potatoes, chopped

850 ml/1½ pints vegetable stock

2 tsp lemon juice

pinch of ground nutmeg

¼ tsp ground coriander

1 bay leaf

1 egg yolk

150 ml/5 fl oz single cream

salt and white pepper

freshly snipped chives, to garnish

1 Remove most of the green parts of the leeks. Slice the white parts very finely.

2 Melt the butter or margarine in a saucepan. Add the leeks and onion and cook, stirring occasionally, for about 5 minutes without browning.

3 Add the potatoes, vegetable stock, lemon juice, nutmeg, coriander and bay leaf to the pan. Season to taste with salt and pepper and bring to the boil. Cover and simmer for about 30 minutes until all the vegetables are very soft.

4 Cool the soup a little. Remove and discard the bay leaf and then press the soup through a sieve. Alternatively, process in a food processor or blender until smooth. Pour into a clean pan.

5 Put the egg yolk and cream in a bowl and blend together well. Add a little of the soup to this mixture and then whisk it all back into the soup. Reheat gently, without boiling. Adjust the seasoning to taste. Cool and then chill thoroughly in the refrigerator.

6 Serve the soup sprinkled with freshly snipped chives.

# Potato & Pesto Soup

Fresh pesto is a treat for the taste buds and very different in flavour from that available in supermarkets. Store fresh pesto in the refrigerator.

## NUTRITIONAL INFORMATION

| | | |
|---|---|---|
| Calories .......548 | Sugars .........0g | |
| Protein ........11g | Fat ..........52g | |
| Carbohydrate ...10g | Saturates ......18g | |

5–10 mins      50 mins

### SERVES 4

## I N G R E D I E N T S

3 rashers rindless, smoked, fatty bacon

450 g/1 lb floury potatoes

450 g/1 lb onions

2 tbsp olive oil

2 tbsp butter

600 ml/1 pint chicken stock

600 ml/1 pint milk

100 g/3½ oz dried conchigliette

150 ml/5 fl oz double cream

1 tbsp chopped fresh parsley

salt and pepper

### TO SERVE

Parmesan cheese, freshly grated

fresh garlic bread

### PESTO SAUCE

60 g/2¼ oz fresh parsley, finely chopped

2 garlic cloves, crushed

115 g/4 oz pine kernels, crushed

2 tbsp chopped fresh basil

60 g/2¼ oz Parmesan cheese, freshly grated

white pepper

150 ml/5 fl oz olive oil

1 To make the pesto sauce, put all of the ingredients in a blender or food processor and process for 2 minutes, or blend by hand using a pestle and mortar.

2 Chop the bacon, potatoes and onions. Heat the oil in a pan, add the bacon and cook over a medium heat for 4 minutes. Add the butter, potatoes and onions and cook for 12 minutes, stirring constantly.

3 Add the stock and milk to the pan, bring to the boil and simmer for about 10 minutes. Add the conchigliette and simmer for another 10–12 minutes.

4 Stir in the cream and then simmer for 5 minutes. Add the parsley, salt and pepper, and 2 tablespoons of pesto sauce. Transfer the soup to serving bowls and serve with Parmesan cheese and garlic bread.

# Tuscan Onion Soup

This soup is best made with white onions, which have a mild flavour. If you cannot get hold of them, try using large Spanish onions instead.

## NUTRITIONAL INFORMATION

Calories ....... 390   Sugars ......... 0g
Protein ......... 9g   Fat ......... 33g
Carbohydrate ... 15g   Saturates ...... 14g

5–10 mins    40–45 mins

### SERVES 4

## I N G R E D I E N T S

50 g/1¾ oz pancetta, diced

1 tbsp olive oil

4 large, white onions, thinly sliced into rings

3 garlic cloves, chopped

850 ml/1½ pints hot chicken or ham stock

4 slices ciabatta or other Italian bread

3 tbsp butter

75 g/2¾ oz Gruyère or Cheddar cheese, grated

salt and pepper

1 Cook the pancetta in a dry frying pan for 3–4 minutes or until it begins to brown. Remove the pancetta from the pan and set aside until required.

2 Add the oil to the pan. Cook the onions and garlic over a high heat for about 4 minutes. Lower the heat, cover and cook for 15 minutes or until lightly caramelised.

3 Add the stock to the pan and bring to the boil. Lower the heat and leave to simmer, covered, for about 10 minutes.

4 Toast the slices of ciabatta on both sides under a preheated grill for about 2–3 minutes or until golden. Spread the ciabatta with butter and top with the grated cheese. Cut the bread into bite-sized pieces.

5 Add the reserved pancetta to the soup and season to taste with salt and pepper. Pour into 4 soup bowls and top with the toasted bread.

## COOK'S TIP

Pancetta is similar to bacon, but it is air- and salt-cured for about 6 months. Pancetta is available from most delicatessens and some large supermarkets. If you cannot obtain pancetta, use unsmoked bacon instead.

# Tomato & Red Pepper Soup

Sweet red peppers and tangy tomatoes are blended together in this smooth vegetable soup to make a perfect starter or light lunch.

## NUTRITIONAL INFORMATION

Calories . . . . . . . .52    Sugars . . . . . . . . .9g
Protein . . . . . . . . .3g    Fat . . . . . . . . . .0.4g
Carbohydrate . . .10g    Saturates . . . . . .0g

 1½ hrs    35 mins

### SERVES 4

## I N G R E D I E N T S

2 large red peppers

1 large onion, chopped

2 celery sticks, trimmed and chopped

1 garlic clove, crushed

600 ml/1 pint fresh vegetable stock

2 bay leaves

800 g/1 lb 12 oz canned plum tomatoes

salt and pepper

2 spring onions, finely shredded, to garnish

fresh crusty bread, to serve

  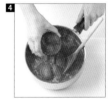

1 Preheat the grill to hot. Halve and deseed the red peppers, arrange them on the grill rack and cook, turning occasionally, for 8–10 minutes until softened and charred.

2 Let the red peppers cool slightly, then carefully peel off the charred skins. Reserve a small piece of red pepper flesh for garnish, chop the rest and place in a large saucepan.

3 Mix in the onion, celery and garlic. Add the stock and bay leaves. Bring to the boil, cover and simmer for about 15 minutes. Remove from the heat.

4 Lift out the bay leaves from the pan and discard them. Stir in the tomatoes and then transfer to a blender. Process for a few seconds until smooth. Return to the pan.

5 Season to taste and heat for about 3–4 minutes until piping hot. Ladle into warm bowls and garnish with the reserved red pepper cut into strips and the spring onions. Serve with fresh crusty bread.

### COOK'S TIP

If you prefer a coarser, more robust soup, lightly mash the tomatoes with a wooden spoon and omit the blending process in step 4.

# Yogurt & Spinach Soup

Whole young spinach leaves add vibrant colour to this unusual soup.
Serve with warm crusty bread for a nutritious light meal.

## NUTRITIONAL INFORMATION

Calories ........227  Sugars ........13g
Protein ........14g  Fat ...........7g
Carbohydrate ...29g  Saturates ......2g

 15 mins       30 mins

### SERVES 4

## INGREDIENTS

600 ml/1 pint chicken stock

4 tbsp long-grain rice, rinsed and drained

4 tbsp water

1 tbsp cornflour

600 ml/1 pint low-fat natural yogurt

3 egg yolks, lightly beaten

juice of 1 lemon

350 g/12 oz young spinach leaves, washed and drained

salt and pepper

warm crusty bread, to serve

1 Pour the stock into a large saucepan, season and bring to the boil. Add the rice and simmer for 10 minutes until barely cooked. Remove from the heat.

2 Combine the water and cornflour to make a smooth paste. Pour the yogurt into a second pan and stir in the cornflour mixture. Set the pan over a low heat and bring the yogurt to the boil, stirring with a wooden spoon in one direction only. This will stabilise the yogurt and prevent it separating or curdling on contact with the hot stock. When the yogurt has reached boiling point, stand the pan on a heat diffuser and simmer gently for 10 minutes. Remove the pan from the heat and set the mixture aside to cool slightly, then stir in the beaten egg yolks.

3 Pour the yogurt mixture into the stock, stir in the lemon juice and stir to blend thoroughly. Keep the soup warm but do not let it boil.

4 Blanch the washed and drained spinach leaves in a large saucepan of boiling, salted water for 2-3 minutes until they begin to soften but have not wilted. Tip the spinach into a colander, drain well and stir it into the soup. Warm through. Taste the soup and adjust the seasoning if necessary. Remove from the heat and serve immediately in wide, shallow soup dishes, with warm crusty bread.

# Mushroom & Ginger Soup

Thai soups are very quickly and easily put together, and are cooked so that each ingredient can still be tasted in the finished dish.

## NUTRITIONAL INFORMATION

Calories . . . . . . . .74   Sugars . . . . . . . . .1g
Protein . . . . . . . . .3g   Fat . . . . . . . . . . .3g
Carbohydrate . . . .9g   Saturates . . . . .0.4g

 🍲 1½ hrs   🕐 15 mins

### SERVES 4

## I N G R E D I E N T S

25 g/1 oz dried Chinese mushrooms or
    125 g/4½ oz field or chestnut mushrooms

1 litre/1¾ pints hot vegetable stock

125 g/4½ oz thread egg noodles

2 tsp sunflower oil

3 garlic cloves, crushed

2.5-cm/1-inch piece root ginger,
    finely shredded

½ tsp mushroom ketchup

1 tsp light soy sauce

125 g/4½ oz beansprouts

fresh coriander leaves, to garnish

1 Soak the dried Chinese mushrooms (if using) for at least 30 minutes in 300 ml/10 fl oz of the hot vegetable stock. Remove all the mushroom stalks and discard, then slice the mushrooms. Reserve the stock.

2 Cook the noodles for 2–3 minutes in boiling water. Drain and rinse. Set them aside.

3 Heat the oil over a high heat in a wok or large, heavy frying pan. Add the garlic and ginger, stir and add the mushrooms. Stir over a high heat for 2 minutes.

4 Add the remaining vegetable stock with the reserved stock and bring to the boil. Add the mushroom ketchup and soy sauce.

5 Stir in the beansprouts and cook until tender. Put some noodles in each bowl and ladle the soup on top. Garnish with coriander leaves and serve immediately.

## COOK'S TIP

Rice noodles contain no fat
and are ideal for anyone on
a low-fat diet.

# Brown Lentil & Pasta Soup

In Italy, this soup is called Minestrade Lentiche. A minestra is a soup cooked with pasta; here, farfalline, a small bow-shaped variety, is used.

## NUTRITIONAL INFORMATION

Calories ....... 225   Sugars ........ 1g
Protein ....... 13g   Fat ........... 8g
Carbohydrate ... 27g   Saturates ...... 3g

🥘 5 mins        ⏲ 25 mins

### SERVES 4

## INGREDIENTS

4 rashers lean bacon, cut into small squares

1 onion, chopped

2 garlic cloves, crushed

2 celery sticks, chopped

50 g/1¾ oz farfalline or spaghetti, broken into small pieces

400 g/14 oz canned brown lentils, drained

1.2 litres/2 pints hot ham or vegetable stock

2 tbsp chopped fresh mint

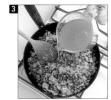

1 Place the bacon in a large, dry frying pan together with the onions, garlic and celery. Cook for 4–5 minutes, stirring, until the onion is tender and the bacon is just beginning to brown.

2 Add the pasta to the frying pan and cook, stirring, for about 1 minute.

3 Add the brown lentils and stock and bring the mixture to the boil. Lower the heat and leave to simmer for about 12–15 minutes or until the pasta is tender.

4 Remove the frying pan from the heat and stir in the chopped fresh mint.

5 Transfer the soup to warm soup bowls and serve immediately.

### COOK'S TIP

If you prefer to use dried lentils, add the stock before the pasta and cook for 1–1¼ hours until the lentils are tender. Add the pasta and cook for another 12–15 minutes.

# Spicy Dhal & Carrot Soup

This delicious, warming and nutritious soup includes a selection of spices to give it a 'kick'. It is simple to make and extremely good to eat.

### NUTRITIONAL INFORMATION

Calories .......173  Sugars ........11g
Protein .........9g  Fat ..........5g
Carbohydrate ...24g  Saturates ......1g

 15 mins    45 mins

### SERVES 6

## I N G R E D I E N T S

125 g/4½ oz split red lentils

1.2 litres/2 pints vegetable stock

350 g/12 oz carrots, peeled and sliced

2 onions, peeled and chopped

250 g/9 oz canned chopped tomatoes

2 garlic cloves, peeled and chopped

2 tbsp vegetable ghee or oil

1 tsp ground cumin

1 tsp ground coriander

1 fresh green chilli, deseeded and chopped, or 1 tsp ground chilli

½ tsp ground turmeric

1 tbsp lemon juice

salt

300 ml/10 fl oz skimmed milk

2 tbsp chopped fresh coriander

natural yogurt, to serve

1 Place the lentils in a sieve and rinse well under cold running water. Drain them thoroughly and place in a large pan with 850 ml/1½ pints of the vegetable stock, and the carrots, onions, tomatoes and garlic. Bring the mixture to the boil, lower the heat, cover and simmer for 30 minutes.

2 Meanwhile, heat the ghee or oil in a small pan, add the cumin, coriander, chilli and turmeric and cook gently for 1 minute.

3 Remove from the heat and stir in the lemon juice and salt to taste.

4 Purée the soup in batches in a blender or food processor. Return the soup to the pan, add the spice mixture and the remaining 300 ml/10 fl oz stock or water and simmer for 10 minutes.

5 Add the milk to the soup and adjust the seasoning according to taste.

6 Stir in the chopped coriander and reheat gently. Serve hot with a swirl of yogurt.

# Broad Bean & Mint Soup

Fresh broad beans are best for this delicious soup, but if they are unavailable use frozen beans instead.

## NUTRITIONAL INFORMATION

| | | | |
|---|---|---|---|
| Calories | ......224 | Sugars | .........4g |
| Protein | ........12g | Fat | ..........6g |
| Carbohydrate | ...31g | Saturates | .......1g |

15 mins     40 mins

### SERVES 4

## INGREDIENTS

2 tbsp olive oil

1 red onion, chopped

2 garlic cloves, crushed

2 large potatoes, peeled and diced

675 g/1 lb 8 oz broad beans, thawed if frozen

850 ml/1½ pints vegetable stock

2 tbsp chopped fresh mint

### TO GARNISH

natural yogurt

sprigs of fresh mint

1 Heat the olive oil in a large saucepan. Add the onion and garlic and sauté for 2–3 minutes until softened.

2 Add the potatoes and cook, stirring constantly, for 5 minutes.

3 Stir in the beans and the stock. Cover and simmer for 30 minutes or until the beans and potatoes are tender.

4 Use a slotted spoon to remove a few vegetables and then set them aside. Place the remainder of the soup in a food processor or blender and then process until smooth.

5 Return the soup to a clean saucepan and add the reserved vegetables and chopped mint. Stir thoroughly and heat through gently.

6 Transfer the soup to a warm tureen or individual serving bowls. Garnish with swirls of yogurt and sprigs of fresh mint and serve immediately.

## VARIATION

Use fresh coriander and ½ teaspoon ground cumin as flavourings in the soup, if you prefer.

# Dhal Soup

Dhal is the name given to a delicious Indian lentil dish. This soup is a variation of the theme – it is made with red lentils and curry powder.

## NUTRITIONAL INFORMATION

Calories .......284   Sugars ........13g
Protein ........16g   Fat ...........9g
Carbohydrate ...38g   Saturates .......5g

🍲 5 mins    ⏱ 40 mins

### SERVES 4

## I N G R E D I E N T S

2 tbsp butter

2 garlic cloves, crushed

1 onion, chopped

½ tsp turmeric

1 tsp garam masala

¼ tsp chilli powder

1 tsp ground cumin

1 kg/2 lb 4 oz canned chopped tomatoes

200 g/7 oz red lentils

2 tsp lemon juice

600 ml/1 pint vegetable stock

300 ml/10 fl oz coconut milk

salt and pepper

naan bread, to serve

### TO GARNISH

chopped fresh coriander

lemon slices

## COOK'S TIP

You can buy cans of coconut milk from supermarkets and delicatessens. It can also be made by grating creamed coconut, which comes in the form of a solid bar, and then mixing it with water.

  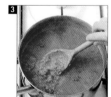

1 Melt the butter in a large saucepan. Add the garlic and onion and sauté, stirring, for 2–3 minutes. Add the turmeric, garam masala, chilli powder and cumin and cook for another 30 seconds.

2 Drain the canned tomatoes and stir into the pan with the red lentils, lemon juice, vegetable stock and coconut milk and bring to the boil.

3 Reduce the heat to low and simmer the soup, uncovered, for about 25–30 minutes until the lentils are tender and cooked.

4 Season to taste with salt and pepper and ladle the soup into warm serving bowls. Garnish with chopped coriander and lemon slices and serve immediately with warm naan bread.

# Mussel & Potato Soup

This quick and easy soup would make a delicious summer lunch, served with fresh crusty bread.

## NUTRITIONAL INFORMATION

Calories . . . . . . .804   Sugars . . . . . . . . .3g
Protein . . . . . . . .17g   Fat . . . . . . . . . .68g
Carbohydrate . . .32g   Saturates . . . . .38g

10 mins     35 mins

### SERVES 4

## INGREDIENTS

750 g/1 lb 10 oz live mussels

2 tbsp olive oil

100 g/3½ oz unsalted butter

2 rashers rindless fatty bacon, chopped

1 onion, chopped

2 garlic cloves, crushed

60 g/2¼ oz plain flour

450 g/1 lb potatoes, thinly sliced

100 g/3½ oz dried conchigliette

300 ml/10 fl oz double cream

1 tbsp lemon juice

2 egg yolks

salt and pepper

### TO GARNISH

2 tbsp finely chopped fresh parsley

lemon wedges

1 Debeard the mussels and scrub them under cold water for 5 minutes. Discard any mussels that do not close immediately when tapped sharply.

2 Bring a large saucepan of water to the boil, then add the mussels, oil and a little pepper. Cook until the mussels open (discard any mussels that remain closed).

3 Drain the mussels and reserve the cooking liquid. Remove the mussels from their shells.

4 Melt the butter in a large saucepan, add the bacon, onion and garlic and cook for 4 minutes. Carefully stir in the flour. Measure 1.2 litres/2 pints of the reserved cooking liquid and then stir it into the pan.

5 Add the sliced potatoes to the pan and then simmer for 5 minutes. Add the conchigliette and simmer for another 10 minutes.

6 Add the cream and lemon juice, season to taste with salt and pepper, then add the mussels to the pan.

7 Blend the egg yolks with 1–2 tbsp of the remaining cooking liquid, stir into the pan and cook for 4 minutes.

8 Ladle the soup into warm serving bowls, garnish with the chopped fresh parsley and lemon wedges and serve immediately.

# Louisiana Seafood Gumbo

Gumbo is a hearty, thick soup, almost a stew. This New Orleans classic must be served with a scoop of hot, fluffy, cooked rice.

## NUTRITIONAL INFORMATION

| | | | |
|---|---|---|---|
| Calories | .......267 | Sugars | .........6g |
| Protein | ........27g | Fat | ...........8g |
| Carbohydrate | ...24g | Saturates | ......1g |

🔺 5 mins      🕐 35 mins

### SERVES 4

## INGREDIENTS

1 tbsp plain flour

1 tsp paprika

350 g/12 oz monkfish fillets, cut
   into chunks

2 tbsp olive oil

1 onion, chopped

1 green pepper, cored, deseeded
   and chopped

3 celery sticks, finely chopped

2 garlic cloves, crushed

175 g/6 oz okra, sliced

600 ml/1 pint vegetable stock

425 g/15 oz canned chopped tomatoes

1 bouquet garni

125 g/4½ oz prawns, peeled

juice of 1 lemon

dash of Tabasco sauce

2 tsp Worcestershire sauce

125 g/4½ oz cooked long-grain American rice

Remove from the pan with a slotted spoon and set aside.

3 Add the onion, green pepper, celery, garlic and okra to the pan and cook gently for 5 minutes until softened.

4 Add the stock, tomatoes and bouquet garni. Bring to the boil, lower the heat and simmer for 15 minutes.

5 Return the monkfish to the pan with the prawns, lemon juice, and Tabasco and Worcestershire sauces. Simmer for another 5 minutes.

6 To serve, place a mound of cooked rice in each of 4 warmed serving bowls, then ladle over the seafood gumbo.

1 Mix the flour with the paprika. Add the monkfish chunks and toss to coat well.

2 Heat the olive oil in a large, heavy-based saucepan. Add the monkfish pieces and cook until browned on all sides.

# Italian Seafood Soup

This colourful mixed seafood soup would be superbly complemented by a crisp Italian dry white wine.

## NUTRITIONAL INFORMATION

| | | |
|---|---|---|
| Calories .......668 | Sugars .........3g | |
| Protein ........48g | Fat ..........43g | |
| Carbohydrate ...21g | Saturates ......25g | |

🍲 5 mins    🕐 55 mins

### SERVES 4

## I N G R E D I E N T S

4 tbsp butter

450 g/1 lb assorted fish fillets, such as red mullet and snapper

450 g/1 lb prepared seafood, such as squid and prawns

225 g/8 oz fresh crabmeat

1 large onion, sliced

3 tbsp plain flour

1.2 litres/2 pints fish stock

100 g/3½ oz dried pasta shapes, such as ditalini or elbow macaroni

1 tbsp anchovy extract

grated rind and juice of 1 orange

50 ml/2 fl oz dry sherry

300 ml/10 fl oz double cream

salt and pepper

crusty brown bread, to serve

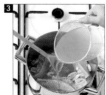

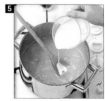

1 Melt the butter in a large saucepan, then add the fish fillets, prepared seafood, fresh crabmeat and sliced onion and cook gently over a low heat for approximately 6 minutes.

2 Add the flour to the seafood mixture, stirring thoroughly to prevent any lumps forming.

3 Gradually add the stock, stirring, until the soup comes to the boil. Lower the heat and simmer for 30 minutes.

4 Add the pasta to the pan and cook for another 10 minutes.

5 Add the anchovy extract, orange rind, orange juice, sherry and double cream and stir together well. Season to taste with salt and pepper.

6 Heat the soup until completely warmed through.

7 Transfer the soup to a tureen or to warm serving bowls and serve with crusty brown bread.

# Potato & Mixed Fish Soup

Any mixture of fish is suitable for this recipe, from simple smoked and white fish to salmon or mussels, depending on the occasion.

## NUTRITIONAL INFORMATION

| | | | |
|---|---|---|---|
| Calories | .......458 | Sugar | .........5g |
| Protein | ........28g | Fat | ..........25g |
| Carbohydrate | ...22g | Saturates | .....12g |

10 mins        35 mins

### SERVES 4

## INGREDIENTS

2 tbsp vegetable oil

450 g/1 lb small new potatoes, halved

1 bunch spring onions, sliced

1 yellow pepper, sliced

2 garlic cloves, crushed

250 ml/9 fl oz dry white wine

600 ml/1 pint fish stock

225 g/8 oz white fish fillet, skinned and cut into cubes

225 g/8 oz smoked cod fillet, skinned and cut into cubes

2 tomatoes, skinned, deseeded and chopped

100 g/3½ oz shelled cooked prawns

150 ml/5 fl oz double cream

2 tbsp shredded fresh basil

## COOK'S TIP

For a soup that is slightly less rich, omit the wine and stir natural yogurt into the soup instead of the double cream.

1 Heat the vegetable oil in a large saucepan. Add the halved potatoes with the sliced spring onions and yellow pepper and the crushed garlic. Sauté gently for 3 minutes, stirring constantly.

2 Add the white wine and fish stock to the pan and bring to the boil. Lower the heat and simmer for 10–15 minutes.

3 Add the cubed fish fillets and the tomatoes to the soup and continue to cook for 10 minutes or until the fish is cooked through.

4 Stir in the shelled prawns, cream and shredded basil and then cook for about 2–3 minutes. Pour the soup into warmed serving bowls and serve at once.

# Chicken & Noodle Soup

This warming, creamy chicken soup is made into a meal in itself with the addition of strands of vermicelli.

## NUTRITIONAL INFORMATION

Calories . . . . . . . 401    Sugars . . . . . . . . 6g

Protein . . . . . . . . 31g    Fat . . . . . . . . . . 24g

Carbohydrate . . . 17g    Saturates . . . . . 13g

🧊 5 mins     🕑 25 mins

### SERVES 4

## I N G R E D I E N T S

450 g/1 lb boned chicken breasts, cut into strips

1.2 litres/2 pints chicken stock

150 ml/5 fl oz double cream

100 g/3½ oz dried vermicelli

1 tbsp cornflour

3 tbsp milk

175 g/6 oz corn kernels

salt and pepper

**COOK'S TIP**

If you are short of time, buy ready-cooked chicken, remove any skin and cut it into slices.

1 Put the chicken strips, chicken stock and cream into a large saucepan and bring to the boil over a low heat. Lower the heat slightly and simmer for about 20 minutes. Season the soup with salt and pepper to taste.

2 Meanwhile, cook the vermicelli in lightly salted boiling water for about 10–12 minutes or until just tender. Drain the pasta and keep warm.

3 In a small bowl, mix together the cornflour and milk to make a smooth paste. Stir the cornflour mixture into the soup until it has thickened.

4 Add the corn kernels and vermicelli to the pan and heat through.

5 Transfer the soup to a warm serving bowl or individual soup bowls and serve immediately.

# Chicken & Bean Soup

This hearty and nourishing soup, combining chickpeas and chicken, is an ideal starter for a family supper, or it can make a snack on its own.

## NUTRITIONAL INFORMATION

Calories . . . . . . .347   Sugars . . . . . . . . .2g
Protein . . . . . . . .28g   Fat . . . . . . . . . . .11g
Carbohydrate . . .37g   Saturates . . . . . . .4g

 15 mins   2¹/₂ hrs

### SERVES 4

## INGREDIENTS

2 tbsp butter

3 spring onions, chopped

2 garlic cloves, crushed

sprig of fresh marjoram, finely chopped

350 g/12 oz boned chicken breasts, diced

1.2 litres/2 pints chicken stock

350 g/12 oz canned chickpeas, drained

1 bouquet garni

1 red pepper, deseeded and diced

1 green pepper, deseeded and diced

115 g/4 oz small dried pasta shapes,
    such as elbow macaroni

salt and white pepper

croûtons, to garnish

## COOK'S TIP

If you prefer, you can use dried chickpeas. Cover with cold water and set aside to soak for 5–8 hours. Drain and add the beans to the soup, according to the recipe, and add an extra 30 minutes to 1 hour to the cooking time.

1 Melt the butter in a large saucepan. Add the spring onions, garlic, fresh marjoram sprig and the diced chicken and cook, stirring frequently, over a medium heat for 5 minutes.

2 Add the chicken stock, chickpeas and bouquet garni, then season with salt and white pepper.

3 Bring the soup to the boil, then lower the heat and simmer for about 2 hours.

4 Add the diced peppers and the pasta shapes to the pan, then simmer for another 20 minutes.

5 Transfer the soup to a warm tureen. To serve, ladle the soup into warmed individual serving bowls and serve immediately, garnished with the croûtons.

# Chicken Wonton Soup

This Chinese-style soup is delicious as a starter to an Oriental meal or as a light meal in its own right.

## NUTRITIONAL INFORMATION

Calories . . . . . . . .101    Sugars . . . . . . .0.3g
Protein . . . . . . . .14g    Fat . . . . . . . . . . .4g
Carbohydrate . . . .3g    Saturates . . . . . . .1g

15 mins     10 mins

### SERVES 4–6

## INGREDIENTS

350 g/12 oz minced chicken

1 tbsp soy sauce

1 tsp grated fresh root ginger

1 garlic clove, finely chopped

2 tsp sherry

2 spring onions, chopped

1 tsp sesame oil

1 egg white

½ tsp cornflour

½ tsp sugar

about 35 wonton skins

1.4 litres/2½ pints chicken stock

1 tbsp light soy sauce

1 spring onion, shredded

1 small carrot, cut into very thin slices

1 Put the chicken, soy sauce, ginger, garlic, sherry, spring onions, sesame oil, egg white, cornflour and sugar in a bowl and mix well.

2 Place a small spoonful of the filling in the centre of each wonton skin.

3 Dampen the edges. Gather up each one to form a pouch enclosing the filling.

4 Cook the wontons in boiling water for 1 minute or until they float to the surface. Remove with a slotted spoon.

5 Pour the chicken stock into a saucepan and bring to the boil.

6 Add the soy sauce, spring onion, carrot and wontons to the soup. Simmer gently for 2 minutes then serve.

### COOK'S TIP

Look for wonton skins in Oriental stores. Fresh skins can be found in the chilled compartment and they can be frozen if you wish. Wrap in clingfilm before freezing.

# Minestrone Soup

Italian cooks have created some very heartwarming soups and this is the most famous of all.

## NUTRITIONAL INFORMATION

Calories . . . . . . . .231   Sugars . . . . . . . . .3g
Protein . . . . . . . . .8g   Fat . . . . . . . . . .16g
Carbohydrate . . .14g   Saturates . . . . . . .7g

🧊 10 mins     🕐 1¼ hrs

### SERVES 10

## I N G R E D I E N T S

3 garlic cloves

3 large onions

2 celery sticks

2 large carrots

2 large potatoes, peeled

100 g/3½ oz French beans

100 g/3½ oz courgettes

4 tbsp butter

4 tbsp olive oil

55 g/2 oz rindless fatty bacon, finely diced

1.5 litres/2¾ pints vegetable or chicken stock

bunch of fresh basil, finely chopped

100 g/3½ oz chopped tomatoes

2 tbsp tomato purée

100 g/3½ oz Parmesan cheese rind

100 g/3½ oz dried spaghetti, broken up

salt and pepper

Parmesan cheese, freshly grated, to serve

1 Finely chop the garlic, onions, celery sticks, carrots, potatoes, French beans and courgettes.

2 Heat the butter and oil in a large pan, add the bacon and cook for 2 minutes. Add the garlic and onion and cook for 2 minutes, then add the celery, carrots and potatoes and cook for another 2 minutes.

3 Add the French beans to the pan and cook for 2 minutes. Stir in the courgettes and cook for an additional 2 minutes. Cover the pan and cook all the vegetables, stirring frequently, for 15 minutes.

4 Add the stock, basil, tomatoes, tomato purée and cheese rind and season to taste. Bring to the boil, then lower the heat and simmer for 1 hour. Remove and discard the cheese rind.

5 Add the spaghetti to the pan and cook for 20 minutes.

6 Serve in warm soup bowls sprinkled with freshly grated Parmesan cheese.

# Chunky Potato & Beef Soup

This is a real winter warmer – pieces of tender beef and chunky mixed vegetables are cooked in a stock flavoured with sherry.

## NUTRITIONAL INFORMATION

| | | | |
|---|---|---|---|
| Calories | .......187 | Sugars | .........3g |
| Protein | ........14g | Fat | ...........9g |
| Carbohydrate | ...12g | Saturates | ......2g |

5 mins    35 mins

### SERVES 4

## INGREDIENTS

2 tbsp vegetable oil

225 g/8 oz lean braising steak, cut into strips

225 g/8 oz new potatoes, halved

1 carrot, diced

2 celery sticks, sliced

2 leeks, sliced

850 ml/1½ pints beef stock

8 baby corn cobs, sliced

1 bouquet garni

2 tbsp dry sherry

salt and pepper

chopped fresh parsley, to garnish

fresh crusty bread, to serve

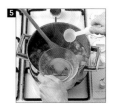

1 Heat the vegetable oil in a large saucepan. Add the strips of steak and cook for 3 minutes, turning constantly.

2 Add the potatoes, carrot, celery and leeks. Cook, stirring, for 5 minutes.

3 Pour in the beef stock. Bring to the boil over a medium heat. Lower the heat until the liquid is simmering gently, then add the corn cobs and bouquet garni.

4 Cook the soup for 20 minutes or until the meat and vegetables are tender.

5 Remove the bouquet garni from the pan and discard. Stir the dry sherry into the soup and then season to taste with salt and pepper.

6 Pour the soup into warmed soup bowls and garnish with the chopped parsley. Serve with fresh crusty bread.

### COOK'S TIP

Make double the quantity of soup and freeze the remainder in a rigid container for later use. When ready to use, place in the refrigerator to thaw thoroughly, then heat until piping hot.

# Beef Soup with Rice

Strips of tender, lean beef are combined with crisp water chestnuts and cooked rice in this tasty beef broth with a tang of orange.

## NUTRITIONAL INFORMATION

| | |
|---|---|
| Calories . . . . . . . .210 | Sugar . . . . . . . . .4g |
| Protein . . . . . . . .20g | Fats . . . . . . . . . . .5g |
| Carbohydrates . . .21g | Saturates . . . . . .2g |

25 mins · 25 mins

### SERVES 4

## I N G R E D I E N T S

350 g/12 oz lean beef, such as rump
or sirloin

1 litre/1¾ pints beef stock

1 cinnamon stick, broken in half

2 star anise

2 tbsp dark soy sauce

2 tbsp dry sherry

3 tbsp tomato purée

115 g/4 oz canned water chestnuts, drained
and sliced

175 g/6 oz cooked white rice

1 tsp finely grated orange zest

6 tbsp orange juice

salt and pepper

### TO GARNISH

strips of orange zest

2 tbsp chopped fresh chives

1 Carefully trim away any fat from the beef. Cut the beef into thin strips and then place in a large saucepan.

2 Pour in the beef stock, then add the cinnamon, star anise, soy sauce, sherry, tomato purée and water chestnuts. Bring to the boil over a medium heat. Use a flat ladle or skimmer to skim off any scum that rises to the surface. Cover the pan, lower the heat and simmer gently for about 20 minutes or until the beef strips are tender.

3 Skim the soup again to remove any more scum. Remove and discard the 2 pieces of cinnamon stick and the star anise and blot the surface of the soup with absorbent kitchen paper to remove as much fat as possible.

4 Stir in the rice, grated orange zest and orange juice. Season to taste with salt and pepper. Heat through for 2–3 minutes before ladling into warmed bowls. Serve garnished with strips of orange zest and chopped fresh chives.